LESS FORTUNATE PIRATES

POEMS FROM THE FIRST YEAR
WITHOUT MY FATHER

BRYAN
BORLAND

SiblingRivalryPress

ALEXANDER, ARKANSAS
WWW.SIBLINGRIVALRYPRESS.COM

Less Fortunate Pirates
Poems from the First Year Without My Father

Copyright © 2012 by Bryan Borland.

Front cover photograph by Benjamin Krain for the *Arkansas Democrat Gazette*. Copyright © 2010 by the *Arkansas Democrat Gazette*. Used by Permission.

Cover design by Mona Z. Kraculdy.

Sibling Rivalry Press, LLC
13913 Magnolia Glen Drive
Alexander, AR 72002

www.siblingrivalrypress.com
info@siblingrivalrypress.com

ISBN: 978-1-937420-24-6
Library of Congress Control No.: 2012909268
First Sibling Rivalry Press Edition, November 2012

To My Mother

CONTENTS

Instructions on How to Approach the Bereaved   15

Dark Horse   16

Those Earliest Dawns   18

Christmas Day   19

Social Network Obituary   20

The Morning I Read Whitman   21
to Three Hundred People

My Companion Piece   22

The Year of Coincidences and Synchronicities   23

Saturdays Before My Birth   24

The Day I Break the First Commandment   25

Recalling a Last Conversation   26
Between Father and Son

Dream Journal, 26 December   27

The Night of Inappropriate Laughter   28

Your Birthday   29

Car Crashes Are My Family's Cancer   30

Valentine's Day   32

The Lady Chablis   33

The Day I Kiss Science Goodbye   34

How Your Explorer Ended Up in the Lake   35

Dream Journal, 30 December   36

On Being Intimate in the Company of Ghosts   37

The Day a Man Asks My Mother on a Date   38

The Day I Pack His Things   39

Mergers and Acquisitions 40

Introducing a Grandson to His Grandfather 41

The Day I Find My Father's Lost Wedding Ring 42

Phantom Limbs of Family Trees 43

Reasons My Father Did Not Commit Suicide 44

A Study on the Grieving Habits of Humans 45

The Nights I Think of My Brother 46

Memorial Day 47

The Days I Believe 48

Long Division 49

There's Talk of Selling the House 50

In the Doctor's Office Waiting Room 52

The Night Before Father's Day 53

Father's Day 54

The Night I Fight with My Husband 55

The Day I Start My Business 56

The Fourth of July 57

The Morning I Stare at the Water for Hours 58

The Day We Do Not Choose Your Headstone 59

The Day I Return to My Wanton Ways 60

Arkansas Post and Other Battles 61
of the Civil War

The Day My Mother Says She Wants to Move 62

The Words We Choose 63

Runaway 64

The Day I Cross the Bridge 65

The Night My Marriage Is Saved 66

Watching *Inception* at the Movie Theater 67

August 25: The Morning I Call the Psychic 68

August 27: Two Days After Mary 69

The Fall 70

Pedestal Days 71

How to Grieve 72

How to Carve a Turkey 73

Dream Journal, 26 November 74

Spared 75

The Day Cemeteries Change 76

Winter Approaches 77

The Nights I Do Not Write Thank You Notes 78

Survivors' Guilt 80

What I Want You to Know 81

Acknowledgements 82

About the Cover 83

About the Poet & Press 87

Alexander (b. 1756, North Carolina)
son of Archibald

John (b. 1785, North Carolina)
son of Alexander

Quintillion (b. 1814, Georgia)
son of John

James (b. 1856, Alabama)
son of Quintillion

Cullen (b. 1886, Arkansas)
son of James

Hilburn (b. 1920, Arkansas)
son of Cullen

Jimmy (b. 1948, Arkansas)
son of Hilburn

Bryan (b. 1979, Arkansas)
son of Jimmy.

LESS
FORTUNATE
PIRATES

POEMS FROM THE FIRST YEAR
WITHOUT MY FATHER

INSTRUCTIONS ON HOW TO APPROACH THE BEREAVED

Do not dance around
the dead elephant in the room.

Do look over your words in the mirror
and remove the last sentence
before it leaves your mouth.

Simplicity is always best.

Do look them in the eyes and say
I'm sorry for your loss

and

Please let me know if you need anything

even if
you secretly hope
they won't.

DARK HORSE

Vice Presidents and sons take oaths
to circumstances they don't think they'll see:
a bullet navigating the channels of patriarchal brains,
forefathers assassinated by black-cloaked conspirators,
death to legislative bills that would grant their boys
perpetual youth. This is how Johnson felt
when Lincoln was shot. I am not
ready to be the man of the family.

I am a thirty-year-old infant
birthed premature, my constitution too green
to ascend, toddling in pastures of illegal crops
with no thoughts beyond the weekend.
I am political suicide, the black sheep
of a dark horse thoroughbred stable
with skeletons in closets so fresh
their spoiled flesh still smells sweet.

I am tantrums and impatience from deficits
of attention, a punk with the flaws
of Generation Me. I text insincere apologies
and don't really love and am not worthy
of standing ovations. I am John John
saluting processions of the slaughter,
an adorable child of history's lens who throws
undocumented fits in the arms of the First Widow.

I have not yet lengthened my conscience or
feet to touch the floor below my inherited throne.
I am not ready to transition from prince to king,
reluctant to put away my toys for a crown
and study the office of my father,
where executive orders are issued by decree
for casualties of innocence,
for our young to ship out and die.

THOSE EARLIEST DAWNS

The guilt that bridge must carry,
oh distracted, wooden hands,
oh railless fingers, oh dangerous air,
oh Walnut Lake, stuff of swimming
lessons and dying lessons,
oh dirt familiar to barefoot feet,
oh grandparents' home in sight,
oh them, long gone, gone long
before I was born. Oh family—
oh family plot so close
the dead must've heard the splash,
oh ice, you jagged beast,
a crack for each month, each gasp
of sixty-one years. Oh absence!
Oh grief! Oh none of us alone.
Oh office without instruction,
oh county without its poll worker,
oh mother who now must learn
to pay bills online.

CHRISTMAS DAY

Christmas has died
and is buried beneath
the frozen ground
underneath a fir with blood-red wreaths
but no further ornament.
Carols become dirges,
a sleigh turns to a hearse,
mistletoe brings sympathetic handshakes.
Midnight mass turns
mourning chapel.
Jingle bells toll joylessly.
Snowmen start to cry
in the early sunlight.
Meringues and casseroles
weep on empty tables
where cousins laugh, unaffected.
Gifts will stay wrapped
until August
when they will be
timidly opened.

SOCIAL NETWORK OBITUARY

My status is a messenger of death.
My status is the grim reaper.
My status is draped in mourning:

My wonderful father has died.

My status is an iSoldier at the doorstep
of ex-lovers and college roommates,
a folded .jpg flag in his pixilated hands:

I am grateful for your sympathy.

My status is an .mp3 of bells tolling
to alert six degrees of strangers
that a connection has been lost, that

our number of friends
has decreased by one.

THE MORNING I READ WHITMAN
TO THREE HUNDRED PEOPLE

I give myself space
because my body is a stranger.

I do not control my legs
or heart. My eyes are rogue dams

that threaten to burst
in rainy seasons such as this. My family

was built on a fault line;
there are trembles and earthquakes.

There are aftershocks.
I surrender and am pulled

by the moon to the lectern.
I cannot stumble. I cannot trip.

If I cry,
no one will think less.

I repeat this and blink strength
into the core of my planet.

MY COMPANION PIECE

At the funeral
they called him my companion,
which made him sound less
like my husband than my pet,
my friend with the furry belly
I instinctively rub. These two weeks
he's been the guide dog
to my blindness. I'd have run
off bridges too
if not for his steady hands
as buffers, his muscular arms
when I wake up too early,
and we cry,
but together.

THE YEAR OF COINCIDENCES AND SYNCHRONICITIES

I have to remind myself he's no longer there,
an hour and a half south, when I see the weather
taking a turn for the worse. For the first time
in a hundred years, there's not a Borland
in Desha County—tending to the cotton fields,
monitoring the gin and the farm books. The heart
of the land is how the preacher described my father.
The morning before he died, I moved furniture
into my home: my grandmother's vanity
to use as a computer desk, a four-poster bed
that belonged to my great-grandparents. I first slept
in the soft arms of chopped and fallen family oak
the hour my father returned to them. Things have
happened like this. I could list them, these
coincidences and synchronicities, but for now
I'll simply tell you of how Lucille watched
me from her mirror, of how Cullen
and Ropa cradled me the night
I became head of their house.

SATURDAYS BEFORE MY BIRTH

You met the woman
who was not yet my mother
in January. You married her
in May. You adopted
her son and daughter
in October. I was born
the following July.
Your family didn't like
the idea of a woman with baggage,
but you carried them
over the threshold of a yellow house
with paper sacks of groceries
they'd only seen on television:
your new bride who was happy,
your new children who
were undeniable,
unquestionable,
and whole.

THE DAY I BREAK THE FIRST COMMANDMENT

Like an apostle I pray to you. I picture
my telepathic thoughts flung to Heaven,

my pious words the baseball
in a final game of father-son catch.

You are deity now, as Baptist-
wrong as that may be, your face replacing

an abstract man, an atheistic nothingness,
an impalpable sky of star-matter and nebula.

A grocery list turns holy: a yellow scrap
of prophecy. An old razor becomes sacrosanct.

Your favorite shirt turns Shroud of Turin, and you,
you have shed the skin of a nomadic Methodist

to remain as the horizon of the night, the place
the sun goes when it sinks out of sight. Father,

wherever you are, I believe in you.
These days I worship a new religion.

RECALLING A LAST CONVERSATION
BETWEEN FATHER AND SON

I am angry at myself for not
staking his words to my hollow chest
so that these spaces of excavation
and mental archaeological digs
would hold more artifact. We talked
for five minutes, joking about
mortality and the missing spines
of politicians. The rest,
I'm not sure, layers scraped away
by the trowel of sleepless nights,
dreamlike words hanging
like dust in my throat, as reliable
as the stories we give to bones
found buried in the sand.

DREAM JOURNAL, 26 DECEMBER*

You are
on the shoulder
of the road

changing clothes.

The cotton fields are in bloom.

Their soft-tipped stalks
are swaying in the wind.

You are silent.

The sky is blue.

The things you love
are at peace.

THE NIGHT OF INAPPROPRIATE LAUGHTER

We are at a birthday dinner
for two friends. It is my first

social outing since the funeral
and I am happy to be

among the living. I order food
I will not eat. I am drunk

on medication and dim lights.
When I hear that an acquaintance

has broken her hip in a head-on collision,
I laugh and cannot stop. I find it funny

my silverware is missing. It is hilarious
that my water glass is upside down.

YOUR BIRTHDAY

When I was fifteen
I rarely hugged you.
Those were our rocky days,
when you worked too much,
when I forged my independence
by chopping down trees
in our perfect backyard.
By sixteen I'd put the hatchet away,
learning instead to carve notches
in bark with your pocketknife
and count the hours
until I would leave.

CAR CRASHES ARE MY FAMILY'S CANCER

Car crashes are my family's cancer,
good odds of bad accidents, a fifty percent
chance of malignant steel. Two of us
were ended this way. In newspapers
we are synonymous with pavement cracks,
our seatbelts and mammograms
interchangeably prophetic. We see no irony
in vehicular ads placed parallel to our obituaries,
themselves empty of reference
to gasoline tumors that weigh two tons
and kill us off one by one.

Instead of a diseased breast
or sickly cell, my clan has a history
of blunt force trauma.

My father taught my brother
and me to drive on backroads.
He was always so careful
with us at the wheel, sitting in his lap,
or when we were older,
our eager, high-topped sneakers
pressing down too hard.
My brother's life insurance
bought my first truck, a black Chevy S-10
with a standard transmission.

It took years for me to be comfortable driving
where our blood watered the shoulder
and coaxed the random sunflower to grow.

My father's insurance paid off
my mother's car; we miss the weight
of his debt. I still haven't crossed the bridge
he drove in December. I choose
to take the longer route and listen to the radio,
expecting at any moment
to find a lump in the flesh of the road.

VALENTINE'S DAY

After thirty years
and the death of a child,
intimacy was a late breakfast
on a Sunday morning. Like
most couples who are violently
robbed at gunpoint, there were
contests of grief: who could stay
silent longer, on whose watch
did the boy go missing?
It's not that she didn't think
flowers were pretty; the cats
would swat at them, overturn
their vases, spill their water
on the forgotten piano.
Knowing this,
he bought her candles
she burned nightly for their son,
flames that would outlast
the white of a lily,
the blood of a rose.

THE LADY CHABLIS

Already I think of her mortality,
this kitten we have rescued
from the silence of your living room.
She was your favorite; because of this,
I have sewn your ghost to her
with thread from salvaged scraps
of the pillowcase I refuse to wash.
You realized, of course, that you named her
after a drag queen, Father. You'd watched
Midnight in the Garden of Good and Evil,
and in the minute of decision to feed
the dumpster feline, echolalia christened cat
and it turned destiny for the homosexual son
to become caretaker apparent.
She rests on my chest, allowed passage
by the other lords of the house
who want to hiss but instead purr.
My love for you has been transferred,
trans… furred, wordplay I cannot resist
for you taught me humor,
but in my humor, there is sadness:
one day she will leave me, too.
The blacks of her pupils hold
a reflection of me that resembles you.
Father and son, we look the same to her.
That thought is comforting, but fleeting.
Ladies age gracefully, but they age.

THE DAY I KISS SCIENCE GOODBYE

The woman on the radio
calls herself an intuitive more than a psychic.
She says that in the first year
after a person passes,
the energy is incredible. She tells
her audience, people like me
who want to believe in something,
that one conversation she has with a caller
might directly relate to another listener,
so pay attention. I pay attention.
I pay attention because my father
enjoyed talk radio. Because it's completely
logical that he would send me a message
through the Italian lady who holds court
with spirits on weekday mornings
from seven until nine. Because when she tells
a man who's lost his dad, too,
that it was his dead father who opened
the doors to his car when he'd locked
his keys inside, I nod my head.

HOW YOUR EXPLORER ENDED UP IN THE LAKE

You drove that road a thousand times, a million
mornings and nights. I want to ask you
if you wore your seatbelt,
why the airbags didn't deploy,
if your heart exploded as you approached
the bridge. Everyone has theories:
axle problems, brakes that malfunctioned,
an Exxon cappuccino that burned
your tongue. My mother thinks
you swerved to miss the raccoons she loved
to feed and photograph. Others suspect
more sinister things. I did not ask the sheriff
questions. I said no to the autopsy,
mindful of your life insurance and
my mother's next thirty years.

DREAM JOURNAL, 30 DECEMBER

We are in the cotton field.
The bridge is near. We speak
through our eyes. You tell me
it was your brain, and in a flash,
I see you sunken in a wheelchair
as if that were your future
had you survived. Another flash:
a memory of a house I don't know,
my mother and sister are laughing.
I see my older brother's face, golden
with the joy of a child's wait
satisfied. I see you both younger
than I ever knew. And then
we are alone, father and son,
riding in a car through
an Arkansas autumn. I ask
without words if you know
the strength of my love.
Your answer comes like life,
a luminous *yes*.

ON BEING INTIMATE IN THE COMPANY OF GHOSTS

Missionary is no good, staring up at the
judgmental ceiling. On my knees is better,

only with the lights off, only pointed away
from the photos on the wall. Celibacy is best

but unfair to my lover, who doesn't yet understand
the significance of loss. They are my family

of mood killers, ghosts who only now
wish to school me in lessons of aves and apis,

shadows who cannot look me in the eyes
without fading into blush.

I used to be adventurous, rattling chains
in the dark. Now I sigh and concentrate,

whispering apologies to no one.

THE DAY A MAN ASKS MY MOTHER ON A DATE

She says it's too early, that she won't
consider it. I grind my teeth
and urge the ghost of my father
to scare away the vultures. I cannot fathom
the thought of a stepfather,
stepsiblings,
  stepholidays
    in the homes
      of stepstrangers
with exchanges of pleasantries and awkward gifts,
so I stockpile hammers, screwdrivers, nail guns.
With each swing, I fantasize of shooting them all
with dirty looks, of offering crushing handshakes
with wrecking-ball pats on their unfamiliar,
not-my-father backs. The paint is still wet
in the living room. I have hinges
to replace. We're busy remodeling
with changes I suggest.
Nothing else new
can enter.

THE DAY I PACK HIS THINGS

I pack away the things that remain
in my parents' house, the place they moved

when I was old enough to crave distance.
Now I want to linger, touch doorknobs,

nod appreciatively at sagging frames,
memorize the ceiling above my father's bed.

The house is quiet. There is no chicken frying
in the kitchen, no dog barking in the yard.

There is no Arkansas football
on the downstairs television,

no last conversations, but everywhere
reminders of little, gigantic things.

MERGERS AND ACQUISITIONS

There are times I feel him in my forearms,
my receding hairline, the irregular jut
of my knuckles, my body a reminder
he existed. After long runs, my left knee aches
at femur and tibia, bones that grind together
in old gospel songs of heredity. In the cold,
my nose bleeds. I blame the dry winter air,
but it's the ghost of genetics, these feet flat
and desert humor, these hands that will know
arthritis and the business of a farm.
My mother says *You sound just like your daddy.*
I feel like him, too, Mother. Worrying
about you, calling you every day,
my joints percussion on cloudy days
when fronts approach in natural progressions
to water the flowers that grow
where each of us rest our heads.

INTRODUCING A GRANDSON TO HIS GRANDFATHER

You will know him through your own
sense of humor, the practical jokes
of heredity that make your eyes water
to the detriment of friends.

You will know him through acts
of kindness, the anchor of heart
that compels you to share your treasure
with less fortunate pirates.

You will know him, little Noah,
when a cat stakes her purring claim
against your leg, when you walk
the first of many dogs on winter nights.

You will know him in your name,
in your knees, in your near
tone-deaf ears that hear melodies
beautiful in the absence of pitch.

THE DAY I FIND MY FATHER'S LOST WEDDING RING

I slide it on and it fits.

Suddenly we are linked by numbers
and gold, size-seven fingers and thirty years;

the age he wed my mother,
the age I placed eyeglasses

on his sleeping face
and patted his chest.

I've never looked at my hands
with such terrible pride.

PHANTOM LIMBS OF FAMILY TREES

I am history's orphaned
sibling, the retold story
of the men in my family
and our phantom brothers.
Granddaddy named my mother
after Sergeant Morley Joe Colvin,
323rd Bomber Squadron,
91st Bomber Group,
a nosedive casualty, he
holds our place
in the Eastern hemisphere.
Marshall Borland also
went down in flames, my paternal
grandfather's brother whose
house and bones melted
into the delta soil.
I was myself a younger brother
for thirteen years, before
lungs met clot and Glenn Colvin Borland
evaporated. Now my uncle
knows the emptiness,
a severed limb, my father gone,
the arm you lose, the missing half
that sways in the wind.

REASONS MY FATHER DID NOT COMMIT SUICIDE

There was a note on the kitchen table
with nothing of goodbye, his slanted
handwriting I easily mistake for my own
with the next day's reminders and appointments.

No matter how lonely the office, he would
have never left me willingly, not to
drive the fifty-five miles to knock
at my mother's door and let her read my face.

He would not have had me
round up animals like the Schutzstaffel
rounded up Jews, though no Nazi
would kiss a dead cat walking.

He would not have firebombed
the sheltered life he'd offered. He would
not have hung me with the shoestrings
he tied each morning until I was ten years old.

A STUDY ON THE GRIEVING HABITS OF HUMANS

Today I gave your computer to a friend.
I've given away so many things
that belonged to you, that carried
your scent, that held indentations
where your fingers laid their prints.
I refuse to keep you in boxes
or hanging in guestroom closets the way
my mother holds onto my brother,
but isn't it the same that I pour your ashes
into unmetered verse? That I place
metaphors into shoes
I can never fill?

THE NIGHTS I THINK OF MY BROTHER

Time has fallen backwards into morning black holes,
where even the cats are confused we're awake.

My clock is ticking fast these days, these neurons misfiring
with age and bursting memories,

like standing with my brother in front of the fireplace,
the warmth of it against the back

of my bare legs before school. Daylight savings
brought with it boxes of us together, things

I even forget to dream,
so that when I wake up, and it's still dark,

I pretend his arm is around me
like in a photograph of us, circa 1982.

MEMORIAL DAY

It is Memorial Day again. The neighbors
fly a flag from their front porch. Our family
visits, my in-laws, my mother. And it dawns
on me I no longer can use the word *parents*
in the present tense. These are our holidays
now. My husband cooks hamburgers
on the new grill. The onions I chop for salsa
sting my eyes. When it is time for dessert,
I put out too many bowls, one too many
spoons. After the meal, we play badminton
in the backyard. As the sun goes down,
I clean the grill before the charred meat
sticks to the grates. It is the beginning
of summer. I smell like a grown man.

THE DAYS I BELIEVE

The first time was Christmas Eve.
In my rearview mirror he wore
the Razorback sweatshirt I've not
been able to find. The second time
was in the middle of the night,
a hand upon my lower back, gentle.
I was not afraid. The third time
I was in the same bed, awakening
from a daytime nap. Through the pillows
I saw khaki shorts. I remember
my father barbecuing in those shorts.
I do not analyze these things or
admit them aloud. I do not tell myself
it's the product of a wishful imagination.
I go about my day. I cook his favorite meals.
I set an extra place at the dinner table.

LONG DIVISION

My friends are divided
into two camps:

those who've lost a parent
and those who will lose a parent.

Those who've lost a mother or father
talk in the tired voices of old soldiers;

there is kinship. We could be drinking coffee
together on Veteran's Day. We could be old men.

Then there are the concentration camps.
My Jewish, Christian, atheist friends who

look at the clock, who watch me walk
into carbon-monoxide showers and return

having seen what they are not ready
to see themselves.

The coffeeshop tables
are getting crowded.

The concentration camps
will soon be ghost towns.

We are getting older, friends.
I am sorry for us all.

THERE'S TALK OF SELLING THE HOUSE

There's talk of selling the house,
chatter over coffee in the kitchen, whispers
between neighbors through cracks
in backyard fences. There's gossip
of our friendship with these walls,
how our hands have steadied
against them in times of grief and passion,
how we cowered once beneath a mattress
when a tornado bullied our property line.
Three cats turned to four here, some
trees were planted to thrive, others
pulled up at the base of their puny trunks
by apologetic hands. The value has increased
in time, though nicks have been added, though
uneven lines tell stories of how colors bloomed
at the wave of impulsive brushes.
Birds have become recognizable
with each passing winter of tossed seeds
and plump, greedy squirrels. We've learned
words like *escrow* and *mortgage*,
how to hang curtain rods
and bolt address plates into concrete.
Still, this is a home meant for a young family
and we've become comfortably mature,
the first gray hairs, more money in our pockets,
tender arguments stuffed and forgotten
in bulging closets and under more beds
than we use. We love your body, House,

your curves and curbside appeal,
the way our music reverberates
off your fathering roof, but more and more
we think of hardwood floors. We nurse
adulterous thoughts of a fireplace.

IN THE DOCTOR'S OFFICE WAITING ROOM

I fill the spaces in a crossword puzzle
with his name
forcing answers
where they
do not
fit.
a
t
h
e
r

THE NIGHT BEFORE FATHER'S DAY

Another Sunday approaches. I am
apprehensive of this one, another day,
six months to the minute and a cruel
anniversary of the afternoon last year
when we celebrated in ways I cannot
recall. For now, tradition has died
in my family. I will mark this milestone
by rising early and running
along the Arkansas River,
stopping at some point to taste the sour
plums that grow alongside the trail.
I will think of you, how you loved
the plum trees in Chatham's Acres.
I will love this fruit, too, oh bittersweet
taste of summer, these temporary things
from the earth that satisfy us.

FATHER'S DAY

It arrives like a diagnosis.
Yesterday the texts and emails:
2morro will b tuff
but here it is, another day,
another tuesday, another sunday,
another notch in the wall
to mark off the months. Hallmark
has made today ominous. The crowd
gathers to watch me walk the tightrope
between skyscrapers. They expect
me to fall. I expect to set foot
on safe ground. The truth
is somewhere in the middle,
some impossible compromise
between orbiting the earth
and burning in the atmosphere.

THE NIGHT I FIGHT WITH MY HUSBAND

I think:

I cannot leave him
     because he knew my father,
no man who came after
would.

THE DAY I START MY BUSINESS

With entrepreneurial heart, why should we
be constrained in cages eight-by-five,
working toward another family's mortar and brick?
I carry your genes, these lofty
and logical cells that sleep at night while dreaming
of early morning NPR and coffee on the porch,
of being the kind of boss that tells an assistant
to take leave early on a Friday afternoon.
You opened your office in the spring
and some days went fishing in loosened tie.
You worked late most nights and let me
play secretary in the summer.
In your hometown, people knew you.
It was there you learned the arithmetic of business,
the social mathematics of little league sponsorship
and weekly lunches at The Catfish Kitchen.
It lasted two years before you sold everything
we'd invested and returned to wrestling the clock.
You still managed to send me to an expensive school
though it is only now I learn the economics of pride.

THE FOURTH OF JULY

I remember the time a roman candle
exploded in your hands. The blood
launched like patriotic sparks
across our paved driveway, your pain
another lesson. Before then, I did not
understand you weren't made of something
more than me, more than easily
busted lips and scraped knees.
You were no longer indestructible, not built
from iron, steel, concrete; the things
contained in the bedtime stories
we read to little boys.

THE MORNING I STARE AT THE WATER FOR HOURS

I feel kinship with the waves that carried you
to the bank, letting you rest on a thousand
lily pad fingertips (wet as the day you were born).

I am in their debt, this matter that blanketed you
like a newborn, that held and rocked you to sleep
in time with the pull of the moon. These bodies

are your cemetery, these streams and gulfs between us,
these tides that returned you to the womb
and brought to an end money, grudges, gravity.

I want to know these things, the great unknowable,
the great inevitable, so I take off my shoes
and socks and wade into the water. The river

has a summer's warmth, far from the wintery lake
of your cold and quiet finale. Life is liquid, the current
through my toes, the minnows around my ankles.

You are dust and mud and memories here, the science
that surrounds me, that circles each moment
and ripples toward the center of everything.

THE DAY WE DO NOT CHOOSE YOUR HEADSTONE

We buried you in Monticello
in the plot that has grown
a garden of family, no longer the single
Christmas bouquet my mother places
on Glenn's grave each December.
In the spring we said the ground
was wet, too damp to set a stone.
We have no excuse in the summer,
when the long, hot days crack the dirt
beneath the good shoes we drag.
I am ready, she is not, so we are not
ready. I think it is her own mortality
she cannot face, her name etched
beside his, one date known, the other,
and everything else, unknown.

THE DAY I RETURN TO MY WANTON WAYS

The transcendence does not last
forever. I am human, after all,
and I sink into childish behavior,
impatience, impurity, the colors
of the rainbow I'd prefer him not to see.
I curse slow drivers. I masturbate. I fail
to appreciate the things to which I clung
for warmth in winter. There are days
I do not feel him, when my ego
burns his wings. There are minutes
I forget. When I remember to respect
my grief, I am the prodigal son,
but each time I return, I've moved
farther from him. When a beloved dies,
we wrap them in shrouds of our skin.
Death strips us of the bullshit.
It is life that brings it back.

ARKANSAS POST AND OTHER BATTLES
OF THE CIVIL WAR

Nine months in, I allow myself time
to inspect the horror of what has become
history. You rolled the window down.
You climbed out with your bad knees.
You lost feeling in the water among
leaves and branches, a place momentarily
as foreign to you as southern rivers to
Yankee soldiers. But you died
at home there, like Confederate boys
wounded in the same woods
where they played army as children.
From the distance you traveled,
I know you fought to live. This is
documented and recorded.
These are historical facts
children of the future will study.

THE DAY MY MOTHER SAYS SHE WANTS TO MOVE

is the day she finally picks the headstone,
a standard granite rectangle
that will be delivered in four weeks.
We're in Monticello—at the funeral home—
sitting at a table with a man
who taught me Sunday School
before I can remember. But I
remember this town, the same
as my mother. It is tantamount
to my childhood, a red bicycle,
a yellow-roped homemade swing
from an oak tree. A dozen or more
family pets lay underneath the grass
in a weathered subdivision near
the western city limit. My brother
and father are here; we are not.
I would like to return
on holidays, to have a reason
to drive past the old house
and smell supper. She's decided
to put our names on the back
of the marker, underneath *Our Children*.
I am pleased. I like the thought
of our family existing forever here.

THE WORDS WE CHOOSE

BE HAPPY

like you'd find in a fortune cookie
    like a morning in a boat
        like a winning lottery ticket
        like a proud parent
    like an Eastern philosophy
like an off-key show tune
    like pie for breakfast
        like an early Sunday drive
        like peanuts in a Coke
    like a twenty in the mail
like hitting a tennis ball
    like taking your son sledding
        like words to live by
        like words to die by
    like the answer to a question
like the chorus to a song

RUNAWAY

The possibility of continuance
is no more a stretch than the Christian Heaven
or the Muslim Jannah.

In a childhood dream, I had caramel arms,
milk-full breasts, a husband who urged me
to clench my dress so I could
raise my knees higher
and move swift in the water.

When I'd gone to bed, I knew nothing
of desperate love or unions. I knew nothing
of lashes on backs or blood between legs.
I knew nothing of dogs on the hunt
through an unforgiving Georgia.

The possibility of a stranger's memory
breaking our skin
is no more unrealistic
than stigmata.

I remember the songs
of frogs: hope
and fear.

THE DAY I CROSS THE BRIDGE

It is late summer
when I find the courage
to cross the bridge.

The sky is blue. The road
is parallel to fragments
of my December dreams.

The bridge is short in height
and distance. There are
no protective rails on its sides.

I fight the urge to follow you
with a sharp turn of the wheel,
briefly thinking it's the only way

to unravel your mystery,
but then I think of the things
that I saved, a shirt in the closet,

your shoes in a bag, and
I come to know what we use
to dress the wounds.

THE NIGHT MY MARRIAGE IS SAVED

On the morning after the night
I can no longer fake it,
we rotate the beds like
the hands of a grandfather clock,
the old family frame ticking
from our room to
the study, the old bed returning
like the witching hour
of another day. The love we make
that night is ours, no
ménage à trois with ghosts,
no cats clawing at the doorframe
we've barricaded with pillows. I am lost
in the lightness of him,
in the sheets that belong
to no one else, in kisses alive
with eight years of us.

WATCHING INCEPTION AT THE MOVIE THEATER

A summer blockbuster
to escape the gravity
of your loss:

I am drowning in make-believe
until the van full of movie stars
plummets into a river.

I am eating popcorn and
watching your final scene,

Et tu, Leonardo?

[Spoiler Alert]

      We

            all

    die

           in

                the end.

AUGUST 25: THE MORNING I CALL THE PSYCHIC

She says:

> *I'm thinking of my Uncle Hugo. He passed*
> *when he was 61.*

She says:

> *There was another vehicle, a black truck,*
> *something high off the ground. Its headlights*
> *were very bright. There were two young men*
> *in the truck.*

She says:

> *I see them near the bridge,*
> *coming towards your father.*
> *They were speeding. They were going too fast*
> *for this road. Something about this truck*
> *caused your father to swerve and he lost control.*

She asks:

> *Is there any connection to the name James?*

AUGUST 27: TWO DAYS AFTER MARY

I do not want to believe what she said.
I do not   believe what she said.
I do   believe what she said.
I   believe what she said.
I   believe what   he said.
                  believe what she said.
                      what she said:

61

      Black Truck

           James

He was 61 years old.
        Neighbors know the black truck.
          My father Jimmy.

                what he said

          His friend James.
      Great Great Grandfather James.
James called 911.

I do not want to believe what she said.
I do not   believe what she said.
I do   believe what she said.
I   believe what she said.
I   believe what   he said.
                  believe what she said.
                      what   he said.

THE FALL

Like the ground unclenched its muscled jaw
and let loose erosion and roar:

you were land, you were continent;
you were sea. Not even slope,

just sudden aquifer flesh,
just instant blood magma,

the tectonics of Saturday
giving way to a Sunday preserved,

a compressive splash,
a carbonized film,

a fossilized photo
in the water of my wallet.

PEDESTAL DAYS

The light of loss swallows the dark parts.
Pardons come easy as breath

in the waxy face of difficult decisions,
the color of the casket,

which shirt goes with forever. We forgive
the slot machines and sullenness,

instead hold our own tongues to coal
for criminal tones. We baptize unflattering

memories, dip them in death, and rebirth them
angelic. We even miss the things

we could not stand: without your snoring
we cannot sleep.

HOW TO GRIEVE

Primordial screams are acceptable.
Remind yourself to eat.
Spontaneous tears in the morning
will last several weeks.
Spontaneous tears at kindness
will last several months.
It will affect you in ways
you do not recognize immediately.
Some days you will not recognize
yourself. The stages are denial,
anger, bargaining,
depression, acceptance,
but they do not come
necessarily in that order.
Do not hold yourself
to impossible standards.
Do not tell yourself
to man up. Do not pretend
you have both legs.
Do not think yourself crazy
for talking to walls.
Expect to lash out
at your spouse. When a stranger
cuts you off on the freeway,
try not to chase her down.
Do not run her off the road.

HOW TO CARVE A TURKEY

Here it is, my place
at the head of the table,

another boulder
in the avalanche of responsibility.

How to shave, yes,
how to buy a car,

now I reach for the knife;
I have to kill this bird by hand.

DREAM JOURNAL, 26 NOVEMBER

You want to show me
what it's like, traveling outside
a body. I am
without body, too,
and together we fly
over farm country
toward the early morning sun
in a tunnel of wind
that feels like heaven.
Then we are above the earth,
watching white clouds swirl
over greens and blues more vivid
than I can explain in a poem.
The stars understand
things that I cannot,
but one day,
will.

SPARED

Another one, yesterday. Another sympathetic doctor,
another nurse in tears despite her hardened arteries.

Thus it begins: the planning of death at some unknown point,
weeks or months or years from now; the slow snuffing out

of life; the pragmatic brother with the carpool spreadsheet,
colored cells, who will take dad to chemotherapy; altered cells;

who will police the family meals and remove all talk of disease;
who will scrub his clothes to rid them of the stains

of hospital waiting rooms and fevered incontinence.
Another one: pancreas. Another one: liver. Who will

be the first to think of medical bills in the unmentionable
context of our dwindling inheritance; who will be strong

enough to see frailty. Another one: lung. Another one:
blood. Who will spend lunch hours hunched over keyboards

reading words like *terminal* and *metastasized* and *radiation*
and *the size of a walnut*. Who will rationalize the slow burn,

be thankful of goodbyes, be grateful of the order
of finality known long in advance.

THE DAY CEMETERIES CHANGE

Like a backyard quarterback
I kneel with my bare knee to the dirt

to settle the flowers we leave
against the winds of our absence.

The morbid nature of cemeteries
has died with you. It is family,

this place. It is my duty
to patrol these grounds,

to straighten the silk roses
on the graves of your neighbors,

to wipe the bird droppings
from my high school teacher's stone.

WINTER APPROACHES

An overnight front brings the cold again.
It hurts to walk barefoot to the mailbox,

to hurry from car to office, to feel the bite
of frost on my windshield. The heater

under my desk was a comfort
in the shortest days; again I remember

the temperature of losing you
and do not remove my coat.

THE NIGHTS I DO NOT WRITE THANK YOU NOTES

For the deli tray
and chocolate chip cookies

for the text messages
when you couldn't bear to speak

for the voicemails
when I couldn't bear to answer

for old neighbors
his and mine

for prayers to gods
familiar and strange

for thoughts ten days after
for thoughts ten months after

for handshake-friendships
graduated to hugs

for looking me in the eyes
for looking away

for space and silence
for cards and flowers

for lighting the candle
and blowing it out

for asking questions
for not asking questions

for changing completely
and not changing at all

for normalcy
in abnormal times

for forgiveness
when my good intentions

are never scribbled
stamped, or mailed

SURVIVORS' GUILT

There were days when it was settled in my mind:
my mother would move in with us. Her dog and cat
would join our animals. My office would become
her bedroom. She would raise the window
when she'd smoke. I'd come home
to fried meat and canned green beans.

Instead there was one million dollars.
He'd taken a policy when I was a teenager
and he worked in another town. It doubled
on accidental death. Another policy
three weeks before he died. He said
it was because he traveled.

There were days when it was settled in my mind:
my mother would work at Wal-Mart
greeting shoppers who wouldn't meet
her eyes. I would abandon writing to take
a second job at the restaurant
where we used to dine as a family.

Instead we are comfortable. My mother hired
a financial advisor. She owns stock. My name
is on more bank accounts than I can count
on one steady hand. We are safe.
There were days when we were not.
I smile at the greeters. I look them in the eyes.

WHAT I WANT YOU TO KNOW

We are lucky.
We have mapped our survival
like fortunate pirates.

We have found him in treasure unexpected:
an inherited kitten,
the swale of farmland.

We miss him with a terrible ache
but our lives have fallen back
to the amber grass like leaves tossed in the air.

We've learned taxes and mechanics,
the things made larger
in the sudden absence of a good father.

I asked him
two weeks before he died
What would I do without you?

He said

    You'd be okay.

ACKNOWLEDGEMENTS

"Dark Horse" appeared in the winter 2010 edition of *The Battered Suitcase*. "Instructions on How to Approach the Bereaved," "Recalling a Last Conversation Between Father and Son," "Introducing a Grandson to His Grandfather," "Spared," and "The Day Cemeteries Change" were published by *Contemporary American Voices* in June of 2012. "On Being Intimate in the Company of Ghosts," "Reasons My Father Did Not Commit Suicide," and "The Day I Start My Business" appeared in *Ganymede Unfinished*. "My Companion Piece" was published by *vox poetica* as part of its "Contributor Series 4: Aspects of the Elephant." "Memorial Day" was featured in the One Pause Poetry Archive. "The Day I Pack His Things" was published by *Referential Magazine*. "The Morning I Stare at the Water For Hours" was prompted by a photograph by Gianluca D'Elia and shared at *vox poetica*. It was published in the anthology *vox poetica's inspirations: images & words, collection 3, fall 2011* (unbound CONTENT). "Phantom Limbs of Family Trees" was published by *vox poetica* as part of its "Contributor Series 5: Dramatis Personae." "The Lady Chablis" was published by *The Nervous Breakdown*. Gratitude to the editors.

Thank you to Christopher Baxter, Loria Taylor, Jessie Carty, Stephen S. Mills, David Koon, Ian Young, Alice Shapiro, Seth Pennington, Philip F. Clark, Parker Merrow, Michael Klein, Raymond Luczak, and Ed Madden.

ABOUT THE COVER

*… black as the underground heaven
from which he rose up into my life*

- Poet Michael Klein,
describing the racehorse, Swale,
in an email to the author.

The original title of this book was *Dark Horse*, but seeing a return of over nineteen-thousand titles with the same or similar names on Amazon, I decided to instead choose the more unique *Less Fortunate Pirates*, a nod to the kindness of my father and to boyhood imagination, which both my parents encouraged.

The almost-title remains significant to me. When I was 12, my father took me to the Arkansas Derby. Watching the pre-race parade, I fell in love with a flashy, hot-pink-saddled thoroughbred named Rockamundo. Though his odds were 99-1, I begged my father to place a bet on him. Humoring me, he agreed, but then he did what good parents do for misguided children from time to time: he vetoed my choice and placed the bet on another horse.

When the race began, Rockamundo's odds had worsened to 108-1. When the race was over, to my amazement and to my father's disbelief, Rockamundo galloped through a victory lap. Thinking my father had bet good money on my high-fashioned dark horse, I became rich by 12-year-old standards. I don't remember how I reacted when my father admitted he hadn't placed the bet, but that moment cemented a dark-horse centered joke between father and son that would follow us for the better part of the next two decades.

Immediately after my father's death, dark horses stampeded into my life, beginning when I'd pulled over on the side of the road after receiving the news. In my panic, I demanded a sign from my father. I said aloud, "Dad, if you're really gone, I'm going to turn on the radio. The song that's playing is your message to me."

Radio, click.

Cue chorus of a song I'd never heard by the band Nickelback, "Never Gonna Be Alone," from an album, I'd later learn, called *Dark Horse*.

Two months after he died, I was on an early-morning flight from Little Rock to New York City. It was a trip of firsts. My first book launch. My first author signing. My first trip to Manhattan. The first time I'd traveled since his death. I was scribbling ideas for this book on a yellow legal pad and at the top of the page, I'd written "Dark Horse Poems." I became distracted by the sunrise through the clouds and the hold of its golden-orange beauty, feeling both my father's presence and the magnitude of his loss. Teary-eyed, I returned to my notepad and wrote, "I miss my father more now than ever."

Raising my eyes and looking a few rows ahead, I saw a

man reading a newspaper. I blinked. There was a silhouette of a horse visible from the paper. It was another dark-horse moment, but this one didn't require any puzzles or leaps of logic. It was in my line of vision.

I wrote, "Yes, dad, I feel you." But not believing my eyes, I also wrote, "Ask Chris to get paper," hoping it was the *Arkansas Democrat Gazette* the passenger was reading and that my husband would save it for me.

When I landed, I called home. Chris searched the day's paper but didn't see the photograph of the horse. I asked him to save the paper, and when I returned, I found it: a photo of a young boy riding a carousel. It was titled "Along for the Ride."

What's more, the caption revealed the horse to be the only surviving example of an undulating-track carousel made by the Spillman Engineering Company of New York. The photograph was taken at the Little Rock Zoo. Little Rock. New York. A dark horse linking the two. Along for the ride.

Yes, dad, I feel you.

Thanks to the generosity of Benjamin Krain, Frank Fellone, and the folks at the *Arkansas Democrat Gazette*, the photograph I saw in the newspaper that morning appears on the cover of this book, bronzed a bit for warmth. The yellow pad on which I wrote is the backdrop.

- Bryan Borland
May 18, 2012

ABOUT THE POET & PRESS

Bryan Borland is a multiple-time Pushcart-nominated poet from Alexander, Arkansas. His first book, *My Life as Adam*, was one of only five collections of poetry on the American Library Association's inaugural "Over the Rainbow" list of noteworthy LGBT-themed publications of 2010. In 2011, he founded the quarterly *Assaracus*, the world's only print journal exclusive to the gay poet, which was recognized by *Library Journal* as a "Best New Magazine."

Bryan is also the founder and publisher of Sibling Rivalry Press, which he began with a gift from his father of $1,000.00 on December 10, 2009.

Jimmy Borland died on December 20, 2009.

WWW.BRYANBORLAND.COM

WWW.SIBLINGRIVALRYPRESS.COM

CPSIA information can be obtained at www.ICGtesting.com
Printed in the USA
BVOW030402200213

313706BV00002B/2/P